FROM COFFEE SHOP COUNSELING

99 THOUGHTS

ON CARING FOR YOUR YOUTH GROUP

MATT MURPHY
& BRAD WIDSTROM

99 Thoughts on Caring for Your Youth Group: From Coffee Shop Counseling to Crisis Care

group.com
simplyyouthministry.com

Credits
Authors: Matt Murphy & Brad Widstrom
Executive Developer: Nadim Najm
Chief Creative Officer: Joani Schultz
Editor: Rob Cunningham
Art Director: Veronica Lucas
Production Manager: DeAnne Lear

ISBN 978-0-7644-7611-2

10 9 8 7 6 5 4 3 2   20 19 18 17 16 15 14 13 12

Printed in the United States of America.

DEDICATION

Looking back it's clear to me how God has shaped my life from a hurting childhood into one where I am called to help hurting teens and their families. Thanks to my family for raising me up as a child in the way I ought to go; to the many pastors who demonstrated pastoral caregiving in my life, especially Pastor Jim and Pastor Adams; to Pastor Dan who recognized a higher calling in my life and gave me direction enabling me to become an excellent youth pastor and to Galilee Baptist Church, the first church who put their faith in me by hiring me. Finally, to my wife, who compliments every one of my imperfections and encourages me every day of my life.

–Matt

Thanks to my wife, Sandy, and my kids, Lindsey and Christine, for helping create our home as a sanctuary where we can retreat from the many demands that call out our gifts as caregivers in a hurting world.

–Brad

CONTENTS

3 Thoughts on Caring for Caregivers

SECTION TWO: SKILLED TO CARE
(EQUIPPING YOURSELF AS A CAREGIVER)

5 Commands for Day-to-Day Caregiving

5 Ways to Grow Your Skills

5 Caregiving Truths to Remember

7 Habits That Show You Care

3 Responsibilities Regarding Physical Touch

SECTION THREE: CARING LIFESTYLE (ROUTINE CARE)

6 Strategies to Strengthen Your Caregiving

4 Proactive Tips for Promoting Health

4 Reflections on "Normal Issues" of Adolescence

SECTION FOUR: SPECIFIC INTERVENTIONS (SIGNIFICANT ISSUES)

6 Issues You May Face

2 Places With Powerful Ministry Potential

4 Reflections on Loss Through Death

6 Sex Topics You Can't Ignore

SECTION FIVE: SKILLED RESPONSE (CRISIS MOMENTS)

6 Keys to Crisis Response

5 Thoughts on Suicides and Suicidal Behavior

Helping Students Through 5 Other Kinds of Crises

11 Lessons from Columbine: Thoughts on Responding to School Crises

INTRODUCTION

It happened again last night. While unwinding after a busy day, the phone rang. I (Brad) really didn't have the time or energy to answer, but I did. Good thing. One of my students was experiencing a crisis. At that moment, I really did not feel prepared or ready to engage. What did I have to give him? Over the next 20 minutes, though, I was privileged to step into this student's life in a redemptive way. After praying, I hung up, knowing that God had allowed me to be part of something sacred. God worked through me to bring the caring, healing, ministering touch of the Holy Spirit.

You've been there, too. We don't have to work with teenagers for very long before we're thrust into the role of caring for their deep needs. It's not a matter of *if*—it's *when* we'll be called upon to engage. Sometimes this takes place informally in the local coffee shop; other times it could be in a hospital or at the scene of a major crisis. Sometimes it's routine, ongoing involvement and care; sometimes we must offer care in an emergency.

And like us, you've probably questioned your preparation and adequacy to be the kind of caregiver your students need. We still feel this way, even after a combined 45 years of training and youth ministry experience. Our knees knock, our pulses rise, we throw up one of those desperate "help me God" prayers—and then we jump in, knowing that with God as our helper, we can make a difference.

It is our hope and prayer that these thoughts both free you and equip you the next time you receive one of those calls or find yourself in a caregiving situation—free you to know that with God's help you do have what it takes to care and minister in his name, and equip you to a higher level of skill and feeling of adequacy. All for the health of our students and for the sake of God's kingdom.

In this book we attempt to alternate "he" and "she" rather than use "he or she" language. So when you see us write "he" or "she," remember that it usually can mean a student of either gender.

CREATED TO CARE

WHO YOU ARE AS A CAREGIVER

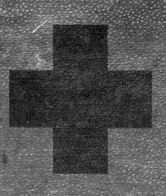

3 Essential Cornerstones

Who you are as a follower of Christ is of first importance. Before we can be effective as caregivers, we must be in right relationship with God, with God working in and through us as we come alongside others. Here are three keys to maintaining your spiritual health:

 ## Stay in God's Word

The Bible does not include step-by-step instructions for coming alongside people in need of care, yet it is chock-full of truths, principles, instructions, warnings, challenges, and examples that, if studied and followed, will increase our ministry effectiveness. The Bible is a window to the heart of God, reflecting back into our own souls, opening our eyes to the needs of those around us, and helping to lead them into spiritual health and right relationship with God.

 ## 2 Depend on prayer

The 19th-century preacher Charles Spurgeon penned these words: "Prayer is the slender nerve that moveth the muscles of omnipotence....Nothing is too hard for the God that created the heavens and the earth."[1] God is the creator. God knows us and knows the people we come alongside to serve. God knows the needs, the issues, and the answers. Ask for God's wisdom—and muscles!—as you enter your role as a youth worker and caregiver. And because prayer is important, why not stack the deck? Don't only be prayed up; be prayed over! Surround yourself with people that will commit to pray for you. Keep them updated with your personal and ministry needs. Lots of "slender nerves" working together are even more apt to move "the muscles of omnipotence." If you're in a key leadership role, send out monthly and weekly updates. Share prayer needs as well as updates from previous communications. Maintain a short list of those you can call or text for immediate, critical needs. Just remember to maintain confidentiality when needed regarding specific students and their needs.

Minister in God's Spirit

The Apostle Paul was quick to point out in numerous passages that it was the Spirit of God working through him that led to his ministry success. We must realize the same. Remember Popeye the Sailor, who was able to overcome great odds and defeat vicious enemies once he had eaten his spinach? Think of the Holy Spirit as our spiritual spinach. Without the Spirit, we are working only in our strength. When the Holy Spirit comes alongside to minister through us, we truly minister in God's wisdom and power.

5 Indispensable Qualities of a Caregiver

The *being* of the caregiver—who you are—is critically more important than the *doing*—what you do. You, as the incarnation of Christ in the midst of the situation, become his hands and heart in the lives of your students as you develop and display these key traits:

 Be loving

Do you truly love teenagers? Do you weep for them? Are you concerned about every aspect of their lives? Is this compassionate love reflected in warmth and unconditional acceptance? This is a priestly role, coming alongside students to listen, counsel, empathize, comfort, and love them back to wholeness. It takes time and energy. The results may not be readily visible, but your love is critical and necessary. Compassionate love, though, must be tempered by tough love. This role is akin to the Old Testament prophet—teaching, exhorting, confronting, holding accountable, pushing, prodding, and even disciplining toward greater spiritual health and a Christ-like lifestyle. Know these two roles—priest and prophet—and know when to use them. Taking on the right role can be healing and life-giving. Taking on the wrong role can hinder the process and may harm your relationship, limiting the opportunity to be a part of the student's life journey. If in doubt, err on the side of the priest, even though it takes more time and energy.

 Be empathetic

You may not fully understand the situations in your students' lives. Perhaps your parents are not divorced. Maybe you've never lost a close friend to death or experienced emotional or sexual abuse. It's possible your life has been pretty calm and ordinary. That doesn't mean you can't step into teenagers' pain. You need to put yourself in their Chacos® (cool Colorado-made sandals that everyone should own)—not saying "I know exactly how you feel," yet letting students know that you hear their words, share their pain, truly care, and suffer along with them. This is empathy—much stronger and more life-giving than mere sympathy.

 # 6 **Be available**

Through the incarnation, God *became flesh and blood, and moved into the neighborhood (John 1:14, The Message).* God was no longer distant. The transcendent God had now come close. God was available, in the flesh. Similarly, we need to be available to our students. Sure, this can happen via social networking sites, texting, phone calls, and other forms of technology, but it's even more important that you're physically, personally available. And remember, being physically present with a student isn't always enough; you also must be emotionally present and available. When you're with teenagers, be with them with every piece of who you are—listening, processing, feeling, responding. As youth leaders, we serve students, which can require the sacrifice of time, sleep, finances, frustration, and emotional drain. Unless you walk away from your God-given calling, this will continue. It's part of the cost of ministry. But with Christ as our model, we can willingly and sacrificially remain available to our students.

7 Be humble

We don't know it all. We don't have all the skills or answers. We mean well but still make mistakes. Realize the limits of your knowledge and capability. Intentionally pursue growth in the competencies of caregiving. And turn to God for strength and wisdom. That's when God can best work through you. Remember what Paul said? *For when I am weak, then I am strong (2 Corinthians 12:10).* Minister in the power and wisdom of the Holy Spirit, giving the praise to God for lives changed, and God will use you as an effective caregiver.

8 Be trustworthy

Don't make promises you can't keep. If you say you'll be somewhere at a certain time, be there! Earn and maintain the confidence of your students. Be a person of your word. Keep confidential information private. If students can't trust you in the little things, they won't open up with the big, important things. Teenagers look to see how you handle what they say and do and if they're safe around you.

4 Hurdles to Understanding the Needs

Even the casual football fan can see that the game has changed. Players are bigger, stronger, and faster. Offenses are more wide-open, featuring more passing. Rules are changing, making it tougher for the defense. Players and coaches must continually adapt in order to keep up. The same is true in youth ministry. Teenagers and culture are changing, making it more difficult for us to effectively care for students. Don't waste time moaning about the way it used to be. Work to understand the current reality, and move on in your role as a caregiver. Recognize these hurdles:

9 Change is the only constant

Culture is shifting; kids are changing. Today's teenagers are not the same as those from five years ago, and they are definitely not the same as you at their age. They think and act differently. They respond differently. Their needs are different. Back in the 1970s, the big problems faced by schools included gum in class, spit wads, cheating, swearing, and fist fights. Drugs, alcohol, and teen pregnancy were just beginning to become issues. Today the list of problems includes school shootings, prevalent suicide and teen pregnancy, rampant family disintegration, and gangs. Become a student again, studying teenagers as a cultural anthropologist would a newly discovered primitive culture. Only then will you truly know them and understand how to come alongside in their time of need.

10 Relativism has become a powerful force

There's been a seeming return to the "day of the Judges," when *all the people did whatever seemed right in their own eyes (Judges 21:25).* We now have a generation of teenagers who believe and do what they want, claiming the transcendence of individual rights over any type of common good or personal responsibility. Behaviors and life choices can be rationalized. According to our culture, there is no absolute truth, so personal faith decisions cannot be questioned. Experience rules. Realizing this, we must understand the importance of joining students on their life journey, not as experts who they'll turn to for all the answers but as fellow travelers who will be there to pick them up when they fall.

 "At-risk" has been redefined

In today's society, all kids are at-risk. This ups the ante for us. We can't just assume that the need for our care is only limited to students on the fringe. Neither can we assume that we can handle all the needs alone. We need to develop teams of caregivers who can minister to a wide range of teenagers facing a wide range of challenges.

12 Students face a variety of crises

It may sound simplistic, but teenagers need the involvement of a caregiver when they face something that stresses daily life. This could be a singular event or a series of events. Different levels of stress lead to different levels of crisis that necessitate different responses.

- **Acute crises** require immediate response. Be ready to bring in professional help. Examples include threats of suicide, school shootings, and fatal accidents. Lack of adequate response may lead to serious emotional or physical danger.

- **Chronic crises** are caused when negative factors continue over a period of time, accumulating to the point they overwhelm a student's ability to handle them. Examples include eating disorders, addictions, and occult involvement. With a lack of response, these crises can become acute.

- **Crises of adjustment** are situations that most teenagers face at one point or another. Examples include relationship issues, disobedience toward parents and other authorities, communication problems, and feelings of inadequacy. These issues, which are normative to adolescent growth and development, can lead to more serious crises if not handled properly.

Crisis Is Self-Defined

We cannot impose our personal definitions of *crisis* on teenagers. If it is a crisis to them, we need to respond to it as a crisis. I (Brad) was reminded of this one Wednesday night many years ago. A student came to our junior high meeting distraught and in tears. As the story emerged, I learned that a car had hit her cat right before she came to church. As a dog lover, I could have easily blown her off, but I wisely realized this was a crisis to her and responded accordingly with love and compassion. What are other examples?

- Failing a test

- Getting cut from a team or not getting a lead in the musical

- Breaking up with a boyfriend or girlfriend

- Being the target of the school's gossip chain

- Finding out mom was transferred and the family is moving to another city or state

3 Thoughts on Caring for Caregivers

On April 21, 1999, the day after the Columbine tragedy, Principal Frank DeAngelis was still reeling, blindly stumbling to put one foot in front of the other. He felt that he had to be strong for everyone else. A friend looked him in the eye and said, "If you don't help yourself, you can't help anyone else." DeAngelis got into counseling the next day, and it was the best thing he could have done. Who he was and how he responded to the aftermath of the tragedy were strongly dependent on finding his own caregiver.

13 Every caregiver needs a caregiver

Don't attempt to make it on your own. God created us for community. We need the support and strength of others around us. Even professional soldiers need to step out of battle to rest and recover before they re-engage. DeAngelis is quick to share that he still periodically needs to return to his counselor, "going in for maintenance." He isn't afraid to admit his need for others to come alongside him to provide the necessary scaffolding to re-engage the battles of life.

14 You may need to be someone else's caregiver

Most of the faith community's immediate response to the Columbine tragedy was handled by the Southwest Connection, a network of local youth leaders. Rich Van Pelt, a noted expert on adolescent crisis response and a member of this network, was out of town at the time of the tragedy. Upon hearing of the news, Van Pelt dropped everything and flew back to Littleton, Colorado. His role, even though he was the most equipped and experienced in crisis response, was not to come alongside and interact with the Columbine students. Instead, Van Pelt became the pastor to the pastors who were in the frontlines of triage and response. This role was of equal importance to direct engagement with the students. Be ready to accept and embrace this role when necessary.

15 Personal care includes Sabbath

You can't keep running on high speed forever. Follow the mandate of Scripture and set aside time for Sabbath. Slow down, rest, recharge. Reconnect with God, reconnect with family, and reconnect with yourself. Turn off your phone, ignore your email, and don't answer your doorbell. The world can get along without you, and you'll be better able to re-engage after time set apart. Take at least one day per week, one weekend per quarter, and two weeks per year for this.

SKILLED TO CARE

EQUIPPING YOURSELF AS A CAREGIVER

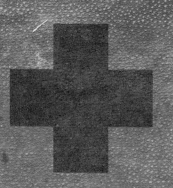

5 Commands for Day-to-Day Caregiving

16 Thou shalt live out incarnational ministry

Jesus lived and ministered among people through face-to-face and life-on-life relationships. Real ministry happens up close. It can happen no other way. We must come alongside our students, sharing their journey before the deep needs arise. We must live life together, talking with them and asking them about their hopes, dreams, and fears. We must truly listen to them. We must share in their joys and their sorrow. Knowing them and sharing the journey will open the door to redemptive relationships. Students are more willing to trust us and allow us to speak into their lives when struggles, difficult times, and crises arise. In Luke 18:35-43, as Jesus approached

Jericho, a blind man called out to him for help. Jesus stopped and asked, *"What do you want me to do for you?"* Jesus wanted to hear the man express his need and desire. In our role as caregivers, we ought to do the same with students. Knowing why they are reaching out to you will help you become a better listener, empathizer, advocate, and caregiver.

 Thou shalt be a safe person

I (Brad) have an 80-pound, strong-as-an-ox yellow lab. Her favorite place in our house is by my feet, under my desk. Yep, she's even there now as I write these words! She feels safe with me, especially if there's a fireworks display or a Colorado thunderstorm outside. Do your students find you safe and appropriately protective? Do you guard their hearts, minds, bodies, souls, and relationships? Are you there during the good times, and can they turn to you during the bad? Do you build them up and encourage them? For many students, you may be the only safe adult they know.

18 Thou shalt create a safe place

We must create a safe place for our students. A place where they can be themselves, free from judgment, ridicule, teasing, and sarcasm. A place where they are celebrated for who they are. In safe places students can:

- accept themselves and who God created them to be

- be challenged toward a healthy trajectory of growth

- be connected in relationships with Christ-like peers and mentors

- give us a peek into the needs and hurts of their lives

- find a place of safety, understanding, healing, and restoration

- flee during times of crisis and recovery

God, the one and only—I'll wait as long as he says. Everything I hope for comes from him, so why not? He's solid rock under my feet, breathing room for my soul, an impregnable castle: I'm set for life. My help and glory are in God—granite-strength and safe-harbor-God—So trust him absolutely, people; lay your lives on the line for him. God is a safe place to be (Psalm 62:5-8 The Message).

19 Thou shalt encourage others to be safe, too

It's not enough for you to be a safe person; this also must be the DNA of the entire youth ministry team. Encourage this, promote this, and model this until it becomes a key piece of your culture. Treat all students as equals. Don't play favorites. Value the life and dignity of all. Lose the sarcasm and inappropriate jokes. Choose your games and activities wisely. Watch closely both your actions and your words. Become imitators of Jesus and wear your HWJTT bracelets (How Would Jesus Treat Teenagers?).

20 Thou shalt be prepared

Be ready with tools for the situations you may encounter. Have a **portable Bible** with key passages for specific scenarios marked or written on a list where you can find them; we recommend a physical Bible instead of an app on your phone because you never know when you'll run into technical difficulties! Similarly, always have **maps of your community** readily available. GPS works in most situations, but how many times has your GPS taken you on the wrong route, down a one-way street the wrong way, or unknowingly into a construction closure? Also have **parking permits** and a **stash of spare change** for parking meters. Make sure you have **official IDs** to verify who you are and why you're there—especially in hospitals, jails, schools, and other places you might go to care for teenagers. It could be a business card, official ID badge, or a letter on official letterhead that states your name, your church or organization, and your role. Consider investing in a **portable communion set** for ministering to students who are incarcerated, hospitalized, home because of an extended illness, or participating in residential treatment. Stash an **extra phone charger** in your car. And finally, **keep a list of emergency phone numbers**—not just on your phone, but also a paper copy on a small card in your wallet, in your car's glove compartment, in your desk drawer, or by the phone at home. Include numbers for hospitals, urgent care facilities, youth correctional facilities, suicide response lines, Christian counselors, social service agencies, emergency housing, and contact information for your church or organization.

5 Ways to Grow Your Skills

Who we are is most important, but we can improve our skills—in fact, it's essential that we do! Just remember to follow this adage: "Adapt it, don't adopt it." Learn from others, but remember that what works for them may not work for you—at least not without adjustments and tweaks. Here are five ways to grow as a youth worker who cares:

21 Grow by reading

If you're the lead youth worker, some of the best money you can spend is on a resource library for your adult and student leaders—and if you're a volunteer, you can help invest in this kind of library, too. Sure, it can include resources on games and how to plan activities, but it should also have counseling and crisis response resources. Search for good books that teach in-depth counseling and crisis response skills. Read these books thoroughly, and then keep them nearby. That way you can grab them when you receive a phone call but you're not sure what to do. And make sure they're available to any leader or volunteer who needs them. Also create a bibliography of helpful resources for students and parents. Include books, CDs, DVDs, websites, counselors, and other helpers. Then put this list in the hands of families, and consider posting it on your group's website and Facebook® page.

 **Grow by watching**

Just as you have your own gifts and skills, so do others. You can learn a lot by watching people in action—even your students. Many teenagers have been trained in peer counseling and response at their schools. They might be able to teach you a thing or two if you allow them.

 23 Grow by attending

Attend formal training sessions at youth ministry or Christian education conferences, other churches, local schools and social work agencies, colleges, universities, and seminaries. Some of these are free; others may have a cost. You might even choose to invest money and take a for-credit class at a nearby college or university.

24 Grow by asking

Be ready to ask others for help and advice. I (Brad) once had a student who we knew was smoking pot and into the occult. I wasn't sure how to tackle this, so I called a pastor friend. Not only did Mike spend significant time walking me through potential actions, he even came and participated as we worked to address the situation. Don't be afraid to admit that you don't know everything. Reach out to teachers, pastors, other youth workers, parachurch leaders, social workers, law enforcement officers, and professional counselors.

 Grow by doing

You can only read, watch, attend, and ask for so long before you need to jump into the fire. Jesus didn't let his disciples just sit and observe; he sent them out to preach, teach, minister, and heal. They probably made as many major blunders as we do, maybe more. Remember that God has called you. God loves your students even more than you do. God will use you and even redeem your blunders. Wisely leap into the fire and care for your students in their times of need.

5 Caregiving Truths to Remember

26 "Pastoral" gifts are not just for the "pastor"

The Apostle Paul, in 1 Thessalonians 5, encouraged the Christians in Thessalonica to become caregivers by correcting the misguided, encouraging the depressed, assisting those who need aid, cheering for people's successes, giving thanks at all times, and praying. In caring for your group, hold fast to these teachings and keep in mind that all of us are called at one time or another to provide pastoral care to another—whether you're a full-time youth pastor or an occasional volunteer. So as you keep reading this book, anytime you see the word *pastoral*, we're talking to you and encouraging you to use your God-given gifts, regardless of your role or title!

Don't wait until you are fully prepared

Because you're a Christ-follower, the living and active Spirit of God indwells you. Remember the message Jesus gave to his disciples when he sent them out into ministry: *"You are the equipment" (Matthew 10:10 The Message)*. When a need arises, go in the power of God, depending on the wisdom of God's Spirit. If you wait until you are "fully trained," you likely will never step out of your comfort zone to minister to the needs of students.

28 Sometimes you must report

It's important to be trustworthy, as we discussed earlier. But we also must recognize that in some situations, we cannot stay silent. When asked, "Can you keep a secret?" it means you are about to get hit with some pretty deep material. In most places, youth workers are mandated reporters with an obligation to get help for individuals who are going to (1) harm themselves, (2) harm someone else, or (3) cause damage to property. We also are required to report when we become aware of abuse or neglect. Assure students you will walk them through whatever they're going through no matter how ugly. Connect with your senior pastor (or youth pastor, if you're a volunteer) and determine who needs to know this information, such as parents or law enforcement. And even in other situations that might not require reporting, getting counsel from other leaders is important. Communicate with supervisors and ministry leaders. Don't leave them in the dark; they can't help you that way. If you have doubt or just need advice, seek the help of other wise adults, your supervisors or church leadership, or your HR team. Getting assistance early and often can help resolve major problems.

 Sometimes you must refer

We have years of training and experience, yet we recognize that some students need help from other professionals. We'll talk to a student on the phone, send text messages, and attempt to meet face-to-face, but if the need is beyond our capabilities, we'll move the student on to the care of someone who is able to walk through the next steps. It is not a sign of weakness or ineffectiveness to refer your students for professional help. Situations requiring referral could include addictions, eating disorders, severe pathologies, clinical depression, and self-destructive behavior. You might meet with a teenager once or twice to talk about these kinds of issues, but we recommend no more than three or four sessions before you connect the student with a professional Christian caregiver.

Develop a Referral Resource List

Be willing and ready to refer students (and their families) to people and agencies that are more equipped. But don't just send them to anyone. Be proactive and create a community resource agency referral list of agencies and people that you feel comfortable recommending. Don't just type the word *counselor* into a search engine and then send your students to the name at the top of the list.

Begin by making a list of issues that teenagers encounter. Once you know the issues, find people and agencies that are experts in responding to them. The best way to begin doing this if you're new to the area is to call local schools and other churches. Take advantage of their community knowledge.

Once you've created your list, contact the individuals and agencies to make sure you feel comfortable with them. What is their expertise? How long have they been practicing? What are their credentials? Are you comfortable with their theology? What are their fees? Do they take insurance? Can they give you the name of a person they have helped that would be willing to talk with you about his experience? If not, secure a reference for them from someone you trust.

If you work with students for very long, you undoubtedly will need this list. Would you rather be ready now or be scrambling then?

Knowing the right people is invaluable

Youth ministry is not a competitive sport. Many other people have the same goals for your students as you do. Have relationships and structures in place before you need them. Get to know the **families of your students**. Call parents. Send cards. Hang in the parking lot to meet the parents who drop off their kids each week. If you connect with families during the "normal" times, they'll be more open to reaching out and letting you in during times of need. Meet your **students' friends**, too. The day will come when they will need someone older and wiser to stand alongside as they navigate an issue facing them individually or as a group. The hope is that you'll be among the first to whom they turn. Build relationships with **key people in your church or ministry**, such as church leadership, leaders of other ministries, people with specialized knowledge or skills you may need to make use of—the list goes on. And seek out a local network of **other youth workers**—men and women who love students and want to be a positive part of their lives. Pray together, learn and grow together, encourage one another, and be ready to serve teenagers together. Additionally, connect with **school staff and administrators**; key players include front office staff, guidance counselors, coaches, principals, popular teachers, campus supervisors, the "school cop," cafeteria workers, and custodians. Volunteer and get to know them, working together where possible. Serve them. Earn their trust. Finally, become familiar with **local community resource people and agencies**: social workers, drop-in centers, residential treatment facilities, children and adolescent crime task forces, park district personnel, youth sports organizations, hospital pediatric units, youth organizations, camps, specialized sports and action venues, and local coffee shops. Focus on people and organizations that exist to help teenagers and to provide healthy places for them to gather.

31 Practicing the ministry of presence

Caring is about being present physically, mentally, and
emotionally—being *with* students during their time of
need and responding in the right ways. "Don't preach or
give simple answers." "Be there; don't do, just be." "Love
us and spend time with us." These answers were given by
Columbine survivors when asked what they needed most
in the days after the tragedy. They weren't looking for
theological instruction or simplistic platitudes. They didn't
want anyone to "fix" them. They needed someone in their
lives, representing God in the flesh and coming alongside
them to listen, to hug, to cry, to hear their story, to feel

their pain, to let them know they weren't alone. If you model this during your regular times together, students will feel comfortable coming to you when it really counts. God encounters us in relationship, not through religion. It's our privilege to be God's hands and feet in their journey—God with skin on.

 **Demonstrating good body language**

Open body posture is huge in telling someone else you are listening. Don't cross your legs and arms. If seated, lean slightly forward. Maintaining positive eye contact shows that you're listening. Additionally, non-verbal feedback helps give subtle clues that you're paying attention. These include nodding your head or slightly shifting your body in a way that shows you are thinking of what they said, are confused by it, or agree with them.

33 Recognizing the power of "room presence"

Your "room presence" says a lot about what and whom you value. When you enter a room, do you normally gravitate toward the same group of people, or do you look around the room to see who is engaged and not engaged with others? Make a strategic plan to spend a little time with teenagers that you need to make contact with. Being conscious of only the tasks that you need to get done blinds you to many opportunities to care.

34 Understanding the love languages of teenagers

Like everyone else, teenagers express and receive love in particular ways. In his book *The Five Love Languages of Teenagers*, Gary Chapman groups these into five categories: Words of Affirmation, Quality Time, Gifts, Acts of Service, and Physical Touch. Different individuals perceive affection and acceptance in different ways. Some will thrive on verbal praise, some with a pat on the back, others by your hanging out with them. Seek to give care to students in the way they want and need to receive it. Your relationships and your ability to empathize with teenagers will improve dramatically.

35 Using your time to display value

It's easy to say "Hi" to a student and then move on to the next person, but that doesn't really communicate that you actually care. Don't be a drive-by caregiver. Don't ask, "How are you?" unless you fully intend to get a real answer to your question. Investing time is a skill done with much practice; your time speaks volumes about your caring priorities.

36 Committing to listening well

Engaging through active listening will deepen your understanding of what they are trying to communicate and will help the other person feel heard. Practice the skills of paraphrasing, restating, and summarizing—in other words, using your conversation to make sure that you truly hear what the other person is seeking to communicate. Also be ready to ask clarifying questions, and do your best to minimize assumptions. Let your listening be an avenue, not a roadblock, in the quest to hear your students' needs and what's on their hearts.

37 Practicing the art of silence

Silence is an aspect of caring that often gets overlooked. We try to have all the answers, thinking we need a quick reply to every statement so that the student knows we're "really engaged" in the conversation. However, this may lead to us cutting the person off mid-thought, coming to a premature judgment, or generating a "fix-it" answer. Simply put, if you are thinking of a response while the student is talking, you're not really listening. As you get more comfortable with silence, you'll be able to read when someone is thinking of what to say next, is trying to find the right words, or is done saying what she needs to say. Looking for non-verbal cues is much harder if your brain is consumed by what you want to say next. Sometimes giving an educated guess of the word the person is looking for can help her continue. The faster the conversation is going, the more likely you'll end up with your foot in your mouth. Using silence to elicit more information and thinking carefully about what you're going to say next (even if you just ask a reflective or clarifying question) will lessen your chances of impulsively saying something you'll regret.

Tip: Practice

At the end of the movie *Charlie and the Chocolate Factory*, Willy Wonka is talking to a counselor in a chair. The counselor says nothing; Willy solves the problem and declares the therapist brilliant! Good listeners have this effect on people. Sit in front of a mirror as you practice giving yourself silent feedback (non-verbal communication). Practice empathy, acceptance, and agreement in the mirror, expanding the amount of time you can sit there. Additionally, practice silent communication with someone else as he does the same with you. Start with five minutes and work your way up.

3 Responsibilities Regarding Physical Touch

Students are desperate for positive demonstrations of love and affirmation, which can include healthy physical touch. This need has become even more heightened as technology redefines relationships as existing in cyberspace as opposed to real space. Yet both wisdom and organizational rules tell us to be careful for fear of misinterpretation and even litigation. What are we to do?

38 Recognize the importance of positive touch

Human-to-human touch is critical for healthy development. A common estimate is that people need up to eight meaningful touches per day to feel attached to and embraced by their community. Positive touch—with or without any accompanying words—can affirm the worth and value of an individual. Jesus understood the value of and modeled the use of touch during his earthly ministry. Be wise in your use of touch, but don't let fear drive you to duct-tape your hands by your side. If your church or organization has a policy in place, follow it. If you're heading off with your group to a camp or another location, check to see if it has different policies to which you'll be held accountable. This principle also applies when going to detention and residential treatment facilities that may even forbid you from touching the person you're visiting. You may not agree with these policies, but you must honor them.

39 Know that touch can be misinterpreted

Touch is best used if you already have an established relationship with people who trust you. Live above reproach, modeling a life transformed by Christ. Discuss with parents, students, and church leaders what you see as the value of and need for positive touch so they know it's a part of your ministry vocabulary. Create a culture of consistency so people know what to expect and so your interaction doesn't come across as awkward or out of place. High fives, fist bumps, and handshakes can serve the purpose of affirmation and acceptance and may be more appropriate. Be consistent with adults and students, as well as with both genders and all age groups, so you're not seen as being drawn to specific individuals or groups. Always be aware of your context: Comforting someone by hugging at a funeral is different from the same hug at a pool party or in your office, and significantly different from hugging in some dark corner of your church.

40 Make sure your own needs are being met first

Your physical interactions with others are more likely to become inappropriate if your personal needs are not being met in healthy ways. Develop close, intimate relationships with people your own age so you don't need students to provide this for you—and remember, relationships with other adults can be intimate without being sexual. Constantly check your thought and emotional life to spot any problems that may be arising. If anything does, seek help and accountability immediately.

If it continues, disqualify yourself from student ministry before you and any students are permanently impacted by inappropriate choices.

CARING LIFESTYLE

ROUTINE CAREGIVING

So far in this book, we've examined some basic traits and skills that will help you care for your youth group. In this section, we'll discuss how you can care for your group on a daily basis. We focus on a series of habits, priorities, and strategies that will help you become a more effective youth worker and caregiver to the teenagers in your youth ministry.

6 Strategies to Strengthen Your Caregiving

41 Move beyond coffee shop counseling

Sometimes you meet teenagers just for fun, making small talk, actively listening, and responding to them as they discuss what's happening in their lives. As you go deeper in relationship with your group, you will find yourself helping teenagers develop discernment and articulate goals for their lives. Negativism is prevalent in students' lives; with terms like *fail* and *winning* prevalent in their vocabulary, keeping the conversation positive can become difficult. Questions that focus on their abilities and draw out their strengths will help them identify what they are good at and will improve their self-esteem.

Consider the risks of giving advice

Except in cases where you are purely educating someone, advice-giving often fails. Why? First, if you give advice and the other person doesn't heed your advice, this can develop animosity because your counsel wasn't followed. Second, if you give advice and the advice fails, you can be seen as unreliable and untrustworthy. Third, if you give advice and it works, the other person may not learn to solve problems and may become dependent on you or other people for solutions.

43 Ask questions that lead to action

One way to assist students in setting a good goal is to ask them what a miracle looks like. In other words, ask: "If you woke up tomorrow and things changed, how would you know things were better? What would have changed?" It is important for them to focus the "miracle" on themselves. They can't change someone else. This question will help students determine what needs to be

improved in their lives and how they can actively work
toward changes.

44 Confront issues appropriately

Whether it be admonishment, reproof, correction,
rebuke, or exhortation, two things are relatively clear
on this subject: There is a biblical mandate for it (1
Thessalonians 5:14; 2 Timothy 3:16), and many people
would rather run than deal directly with a situation where
a teenager needs correction (and jeopardize the title
of "cool youth leader"). Guidelines for correction can
be found in Matthew 18:15-17. This text encourages
us to deal with sin one-on-one. After that, take another
person to be a part of the conversation. If the problem
persists, enlist your ministry's leadership. Always make
sure to separate the behavior from the person. Labeling
behaviors can lead to understanding and change;
labeling students distorts their *Imago Dei*—being made
in the image of God. What else does it take to confront
appropriately?

Don't react out of anger: The Bible tells us that even in the midst of our anger, we must not sin (see Ephesians 4:26). The first action you need to take is to check yourself. Don't react out of anger, don't fire a quick-witted comeback, and don't do anything that you will regret when you realize what you did—or when parents, church leaders, or your pastor find out. If needed, separate the parties who are in conflict, including removing yourself from the conflict. Put trusted people in charge, collect yourself, and then react in a levelheaded manner.

Listen to the complete story from all sides: Sometimes things happen for reasons that are unknown at first. Sometimes what seems obvious is not. It's also a good rule of thumb to start with victims and witnesses before moving to your potential suspect. The perpetrator has the most reason to lie, which will make the situation worse.

Be prepared to follow through on consequences: When warning teenagers, meting out consequences, or reconciling students to the group, follow through. If students see your threats as idle, you lose your ability to hold people accountable. If you have determined and announced a consequence ahead of time (such as getting sent home from camp for violating rules), make sure those with authority over you know and agree with the levels of punishment you want to give for certain behaviors. It's harder for them to be caught off guard if they are on board ahead of time, and it's less likely that they will veto your decision (and neuter your leadership).

45 Help students develop good goals

In your role as a caregiver, you can help teenagers discover the rewards of setting good goals—and aid them in learning how to set those goals. Focus on the acronym SPAMO[2]; goals should be Small, Precise, Achievable, Measurable, and Observable.

Small: Good goals are small; if you eye a goal that is big and requires multiple steps, reduce it to smaller steps. Some goals fail because they are so huge that progress is hard to notice. Visionary goals can be big, but break them down into smaller action steps.

Precise: A precise goal is simple and specific. Vague goals are hard to measure. If someone says, "I want to be happy," ask, "How will you know if you are happy? What will you be doing that tells me you are happy?" Questions like these will open the door to clarity. Vague goals are doomed because nobody can tell when they are actually achieved.

Achievable: Can we accomplish this goal? Can it be done soon? If the goal is too great or success is too far off, it will act as a deterrent in being a successfully completed goal. "I want to memorize the entire Bible" is a ginormous goal. Starting off with a paragraph or verse creates small victories that help lead to larger victories.

Measurable: Can we tell by some measurement that progress is being made in this goal? If the goal is too intangible ("I want to make a difference"), it will be difficult to determine successful completion. However, you can easily tell if you prayed for five minutes three times this week or served in a ministry to the homeless twice a month.

Observable: A good goal requires observable outcomes. Otherwise, it might be a wish, a dream, or an illusion that a student pursues without achieving. Ask the question, "How will I be able to tell this happened in your life?" or "How will X look different after you accomplish this goal?"

46 Establish boundaries for technology

Some youth workers choose to use Twitter for their friends and Facebook for church or design a specific church page for Facebook. Be wise about what you post online; be sure that it represents you and your ministry or organization well. Also, the majority of your teenagers are likely wired, but some may be struggling with it as a time-waster or an addiction. Encourage students to abandon their tech gear during your meetings; be present with them, too, by not checking your phone when you are talking with them. We also would encourage you to avoid confronting online; leave that for face-to-face conversations.

4 Proactive Tips for Promoting Health

"Pay me now or pay me later." I (Brad) experienced the truth of this statement several years ago when my car was low three quarts of oil. (Don't ask me how!) The neglect of a $30 oil change cost me $4,000 to replace the engine—a lesson in the value of preventative maintenance. It's the same when working with teenagers. It's much easier to prevent damage proactively than to help them when they're already broken. Here are five ideas that will help you promote and encourage health in students' lives and in your ministry or organization.

47 Preach and teach for health

Take advantage of opportunities to train, equip, and encourage students into a place of health. Yes, this means talking about the do's and don'ts of Scripture, but even more so it means teaching who we are in Christ as individuals and as a group: our inward relationship (being the people God created us to be), our vertical relationship with God (living life to the fullest as redeemed and transformed children of God), and our horizontal relationship with others (living as God intended for us to live in redeemed community).

48 Create and encourage relationships of encouragement and accountability

God intends life to be lived in community. Help students (and other adult leaders) build, nurture, and maintain relationships with people who can encourage them and hold them accountable. Encouragement is great, and students love it. Accountability is also necessary, even if it can be painful and difficult to take. Lone rangers don't make for healthy, growing Christ-followers.

49 Equip your students

I (Brad) was fishing recently with one of my youth pastor friends. He was moaning about the sheer volume of time he gives to his "needy" students. I challenged him to multiply himself by training, equipping, and releasing others as caregivers—including students. It amazes me that schools are training teenagers and using them as peer counselors, but in the church we're afraid they might mess up and cause problems—even though we Christians believe that God works through people. Take a risk and give students a chance to offer care, too.

50 Understand the MEATS behind behavior

Specific actions and sudden behavioral changes are sometimes explained by one of several factors.

Understanding the cause helps when we are identifying the best ways to assist teenagers through specific situations. I (Matt) was giving a lesson and one of my normally well-behaved youth was being abnormally disruptive. Finally one of the leaders took him out of the room. I tried to catch him after group but wasn't able to find him. The next week, he came to me to apologize. He said his parents had signed their divorce papers. While standing in silence, the only response I could come up with was to just put my arm around him. After a few moments passed, I told him I was sorry for what he was going through. I also let him know that rather than acting out, he could ask a leader to go for a walk with him. Rather than lecturing, I redirected the behavior if it were to come up again. Here are some other root causes behind behavior.

Medical: At one summer camp, I (Matt) noticed that the most amicable students were becoming belligerent, people were upset at each other, and one guy even had a seizure. I failed to realize that I had taken my group up 1,000 feet in elevation and had them running around in hot weather in full sunlight. They were dehydrated, which caused changes in their behaviors. The only way to solve this problem was to get them out of the sun and make sure they were properly hydrated. Sometimes there is a medical cause for behavioral change; it might be as easily addressed as the situation my students faced, or it might be a more serious health issue requiring care from a doctor. Consider this root cause first, or else you may be fighting a losing battle trying to treat the wrong cause.

Escape: An individual may want out of a situation because something unpleasant or uncomfortable is happening. I typically see this in students who have been bullied or embarrassed. If embarrassed, this could lead to an attempt to show up the person or people who embarrassed them. If being bullied, this might lead to a show of force to create fear in the other person or a tactic to run away (fight or flight). Deal with this behavior by helping the individual feel safe and find ways to cope.

Attention: Attention has two forms: Look at me because I want to be the center of attention, and look at me because I'm hurting. The first form needs to be addressed directly, helping the student realize that there is a time and a place for seeking attention. One strategy is to help the teenager find a place in ministry or involvement. The second form requires more savvy to detect; normally, this misbehavior or overly good behavior subtly calls attention to oneself in the hopes someone will care enough to get involved. After Elijah ran from Jezebel in 1 Kings 19, God came to Elijah to see why he ran away. Rather than rebuke Elijah, God provided caring attention and sent angels to feed him while Elijah overcame his hurt and recovered his strength.

Tangibles: Tangibles are something physical or abstract that a person wants. People behave in a manner that causes them to get the desired object. Most of us do this with our jobs: We keep showing up, and the boss pays us. We perform in order to get something tangible on payday. However, behavioral changes to get tangibles are not always good. Sometimes this can be manipulative. Encourage the student to fulfill reasonable needs in appropriate ways.

Sex: A major cause of adolescent behavioral problems is sex—not necessarily sexual activity, but relationships, attractions, and love. This can come across as teasing, competitiveness, sudden good or bad behavior, and doing things (often stupid) to attract attention from the opposite sex. Youth workers are in a unique place to help set appropriate boundaries, explaining feelings and emotions to an age group that does not always have access to the rational parts of the brain. Intervention can sometimes be pre-emptive—such as lessons on the subject—or it can be responsive (see our later section addressing several sex-related topics).

4 Reflections on "Normal Issues" of Adolescence

Each year my (Brad) Ministry to At-Risk class surveys adolescents, parents, and those who work with them to discover the issues students face. There are now close to 200 issues on the list: identity, relationships, spirituality, family, media and technology, worldview, sexuality, the future—the list goes on. Overwhelming? Yes, but here are a few reflections:

51 Consider your own situation

Figure out the biggest needs in your community and in your group. Ask one simple question: "What are the prevalent issues our teenagers deal with?" Include students, parents, teachers, coaches, community leaders, youth ministry staff, and other churches' youth workers. Now the work begins. Read, use online search engines, find experts in your area—do whatever it takes to understand these issues. Learn all you can about the symptoms, causes, deeper issues, potential responses, and preventative measures. Then make sure you and your fellow leaders know what an "ideal, healthy student" looks like. A contractor can't build a house without an architect's plan. Where do we find this ideal? First, in Scripture. Second, in developmental psychology textbooks—read and screened through "Scripture eyes." A great resource is "40 Developmental Assets for Adolescents" available through the Search Institute (search-institute.org/content/40-developmental-assets-adolescents-ages-12-18).

 **Band together with others who care**

You're not the only one concerned about your teenagers. Band together for their common good. Networking creates a critical mass of energy and resources. And yes, you can network with people and agencies from the public sector and from different faith groups.

53 Don't be part of the problem

Evaluate your programs and personal behavior. Do they contribute to solutions, or are they creating problems? We contribute through our overt policies and actions or through ignoring the problem altogether. This may even lead to major overhauls. Hard work? Yes, but isn't it worth it?

54 Recognize the juggling act

Adolescent life today is a juggling act: academics, athletics, extracurricular activities, home and family life, jobs, friends, church. Considering all of these challenges and demands on teenagers' lives, is it really surprising that they drop a ball here and there? Empathy, time, space, and minimal advice when asked will go much further than critiquing how a student is messing up.

SECTION FOUR

SPECIFIC INTERVENTIONS

SIGNIFICANT ISSUES

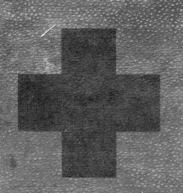

6 Issues You May Face

55 Bullying

Bullying is not new to adolescent culture. A major way bullying happens is by segregation based on difference (bigotry or bias). In an effort to create conformity across their lives, teenagers pressure others to conform to their own standards (or lack thereof). Bullying often stems from insecurity of the bullies and the vulnerability of potential victims. School and social systems tacitly condone bullying by not confronting it when it happens, sometimes causing the victim to lash out against the bullies and systems that condone them. **Cyber-bullying** is a form of bullying that happens online or via text messages. The danger in cyber-bullying is that it can spread rapidly and that it often sabotages the safety in a teenager's safe places. If students can feel threatened and abused in their own home, how can they feel safe anywhere else?

Caring for the bullied: A bullied student needs to feel acceptance. Being part of a group that values him for who he is will help a teenager combat the negative forces instilled by bullying. Help the student work through self-blame by gently asserting bullying is not his fault; it has more to do with the poor self-image of the bully. Encourage the student to find positive peer and adult relationships. This may help stem the tide of bullying that can attack students during their teen years.

56 Divorce

While some teenagers might be relieved at their parents' divorce and the peace it may bring, many others live in a state of denial and hope their parents won't complete the divorce but will reconcile instead. Even if the process takes years and everyone seems settled on the reality of divorce, teenagers can have significant reactions when the divorce is finalized—some needing significant intervention. While it is not our job to extinguish hope or the possibility of reconciliation, we need to be aware of the student's desire and proclivity to hang on to that final strand as long as possible. Teenagers and children also will often look to blame themselves for their parents' problems. If a student shares these feelings during conversation, gently challenge his logic. If it's a parent directing that venom at the child, encourage the student and dissuade him from the misplaced anger. And don't hesitate pursuing a conversation with parents, helping them to understand how their behavior is affecting their child. A major predictor of success for how well a teenager will survive her parents' divorce is having positive role models, steady support structures, and healthy boundaries. It involves caring enough to compassionately confront if a student starts acting out, yet having a firm hand to support and redirect any such incidents. Teenagers may act aggressively, get depressed, become sexually active, experience academic problems, or even consider suicide. Utilizing skills discussed in the previous sections of this book can help you guide students through this time.

 **Addictions**

The CAGE assessment[3] is designed to help people recognize or start to think about their behavior as problematic or addictive.

- **C** = Have they ever tried to **cut** down on the behavior?

- **A** = Have they gotten **annoyed** by others mentioning the issue to them?

- **G** = Have they ever felt **guilty** about the problem behavior or inability to stop it?

- **E** = Have they ever needed the addictive substance to **ease** withdrawal symptoms?

Many addictions require support groups and other help in overcoming. For example, pornography is a difficult addiction because it works with the brain's biochemistry and does not need external stimulants (drugs, alcohol, Internet) to get the high of addiction.

Instilling a culture of change: I (Matt) realized after learning about the Trans-Theoretical Model[4] that you can't force a person into a decision when he doesn't realize a choice needs to be made in the first place. This model will help you understand how to influence a student to make a change in his life. Here is an adaptation of the model:

Pre-contemplation: The person doesn't recognize the need for change. For this person we introduce the idea of the need for change.

Contemplation: In this stage we help the person make a decision to change (or discover how to change).

Preparation: In this stage we help him prepare to make a change and talk about what that change will look like.

Maintenance: This is where the person starts on a course of action and keeps it going. Relapse: This is considered a normal part of the process, where we help the person get past his "failure" and get back into an appropriate stage of change. Two basic questions to ask someone bouncing back from relapse are "What worked?"—do it more—and "What hurt?"—how can you do it less or avoid it?

58 Eating disorders

The phrase "eating disorders" refers to a patterned misuse of food in both overuse and underuse. Some people may occasionally have disordered eating habits, while others get stuck in more vicious eating disorders such as anorexia and bulimia. You may need to enlist the help of professional counselors in this. Whenever you refer, don't abandon the student, but have the counselor take over the counseling while you continue to be her youth worker.

Body image: *Imago Dei* (translated, "Image of God") is the Latin phrase used by theologians to describe the make-up and inherent value of all human beings. We were made in God's image (Genesis 1:27); this was reaffirmed after the fall (Genesis 9:6). Christ is also called the image of God (2 Corinthians 4:4). Human beings get innate value from being made in the image of God and the likeness of Jesus Christ. When working with students, this value enables us to love them unconditionally and to value who they are and who God created them to be— rejecting what the world tells them.

Anorexia nervosa: Anorexia, like many body image disorders, is about a created sense of perfectionism and need for control. Anorexia is often rooted in some abuse or traumatic event that causes the individual to compulsively diet through self-starvation. This becomes a coping mechanism to deal with life. Recovery from anorexia includes having empathic people walk the student through her thought patterns and gently examine her false assumptions. Help her dig into the causes of her beliefs and subsequent actions. Gently help her expose faulty beliefs and gain a healthy understanding of food and self.

Bulimia nervosa: Bulimia is similar to anorexia in that it is an anxiety-induced eating disorder. The person with bulimia copes with heightened anxiety by binging and then inducing a purge activity such as throwing up, abusing laxatives, or exercising excessively. People with bulimia seek control over the pain in their lives, which is often caused by sexual abuse or a major traumatic event in their past. Safety and internal security are found in the ability to control one's eating and weight. Be open in discussing disordered eating in a direct way without being accusative. Empathize but don't condone the disordered eating, and reach inside the discussion to gently nudge the person away from faulty thinking habits.

 **Chronic illnesses**

Chronic illnesses are constant or intermittent illnesses that impact (to varying degrees) a student's health and can limit participation in many "normal" teenage activities. Some of these chronic conditions include seizure disorders, asthma, diabetes, lupus, hypertension, or a long-term illness such as cancer. Most of the ideas we share below apply best to more serious health conditions.

Caring for the student: The teenager may have some limitations and things you can't do with him, but engage on an appropriate level. Ever wondered why pediatric units have video games available? Distraction is a great way to alleviate patients' pain. This is probably the only area where you have a bona fide excuse that playing games is pure ministry! Find out from parents and medical staff what the student can and can't do and what level of interaction is appropriate. Also remember the need for positive touch.

Caring for parents: Parents of a child with a chronic illness may feel a sense of powerlessness. They are stretched emotionally, spiritually, financially, and psychologically as they wrestle with this illness, helping their child have a good life. Steer clear of platitudes and cliché sayings like "You're so strong" and "I don't know how you do it." Allow for weakness, empathize with the pain and difficulty, and encourage through presence and silence rather than always being quick with words. Encourage parents to maintain some semblance of a routine in the life of the family. Also encourage them to maintain healthy boundaries and discipline within the family; illness isn't an excuse for poor behavior, but sometimes compassion needs to be used in redirecting and interpreting behavior of a hurting child.

Caring for siblings: Other children in the home may feel (or are) neglected and often feel invisible. Ways to combat this include spending time with the other children, arranging for play dates for the siblings with friends from church, taking them to a meal, and showing up to some event they are participating in. This will do two things: show the "invisible children" they are being cared for and allow the parents of a chronically ill child the chance to take a breath.

Caring for friends: Spend time with the student's friends. Help them understand the illness, what limits they may have in hanging out with their friend, and how they can be good, caring friends. Encourage them not to walk away but to step up in sacrificial love.

When the illness is terminal: Friends and family of terminally ill teenagers need to work through five essential tasks. They need to be able to say:

- Thank you.

- I'll miss you.

- It's OK to go.

- I forgive you.

- Forgive me.

These five statements are normally followed up with more explanation, such as "thank you for being such a great son." Helping a family through these tasks will help them cope with the death of their loved one and feel like they have said their peace as much as possible.

Hospice and Outside Services

Hospice provides end-of-life care through a team of professionals that most commonly includes a nurse, a social worker, and a chaplain who come around the family near the time of death and help provide care. Chaplains are great resources in end-of-life care such as finding a mortuary, prices for funerals, and explaining what the end-of-life process is like. Consult with the chaplain to help provide care for the family.

60 Students with special needs

At some point you likely will have a student in your group who has a developmental disability. Here are a few pointers in how to serve and care for teenagers with special needs.

Do your homework: One option is to say, "We don't have the staffing to adequately serve this type of student." Another option is to study how to minister to your student based on her specific condition. Ask the parents of the student what works for her. What is the best way she learns? What can she tolerate doing? How long can she endure specific activities? How easily can she be included with everyone—with or without assistance? How much assistance does she need?

Get permission to solicit input from teachers: Ask to meet with the teenager's teacher (or teachers) and ask questions. A teacher trained in working with developmental disabilities may be able to suggest resources that you can adapt to your ministry setting. You might even be able to get permission to observe the student in class to see how the class and the teacher interact with him and what routines help him get through the day.

Educate other students: While in the past people preferred to keep secrets regarding personal disabilities out of concern of privacy and embarrassment, we've found that these secrets often instill fear and ridicule of individuals who are different from the rest of the group. Calmly explaining what is going on with the student and what may happen if she has a bad day will help understanding and can instill compassion in others. Education helps stifle antagonistic behaviors by others. Always discuss this first with the parents and the student,

though, getting their approval as to how much to share—
or allow the student to share details with the group.

2 Places With Powerful Ministry Potential

61 Respond when students are incarcerated

Youth services center, juvenile detention facility, juvenile correction center—the names differ, but they exist in nearly every community or county. And the day may come when one of your students is being held there. Seize the opportunity to visit, without seeing it as a burden. Engaging students during difficult times in their lives opens the door to significant ministry opportunities there and beyond. Here are some helpful thoughts.

Build connections beforehand: We've already talked about networks and knowing the right people, and this definitely is one of those "get to know them and let them get to know you beforehand" places. It's always better if officials already know you, trust you, and are open to your presence. They may even then call you when one of the other adolescent detainees expresses interest in a visit from a youth worker.

Know the context: The rules and logistics vary widely from facility to facility. Important things to know include:

- What are the official visiting hours? Are there different ones for clergy or youth workers? Clergy visiting hours are often different and more liberal.

- What are the requirements for you to visit? Parental permission? Your name on an official list? Specialized credentials or training?

- What can you bring, and what is banned?

- What are the rules regarding physical contact?

- Are there different policies for visiting detained, adjudicated, or committed adolescents? Talk with officials or connect with local ministries that serve jails and prisons so you can understand the "insider" language and procedures.

Know your role: Encourage; don't preach or condemn. Teenagers usually know they've messed up if they're now in a detention facility. Show unconditional love and acceptance. This teenager needs someone in his corner—neither condemning nor condoning his actions—but listening, loving, and letting him know he has potential to be so much more. Focus on building a relationship that the teenager may pursue when he's released. Open the door to spiritual conversation, but don't force your way in. Offer to pray for him—while there and after you've left. But remember your responsibilities—what you must keep confidential and what you can't.

Don't ignore other players: Family, friends, youth groups—who else is impacted by this student's detainment? Do they need someone interacting with them at this time? If you are not able or are not the right person to connect with them, find someone who can get involved. It may be a role of encouragement or may be assisting with practical needs like providing rides or offering childcare help so family can visit the teenager. Also, help other students figure out how they can be involved. They probably can't visit, but they can write, pray, and even attend public trials as encouragers, letting the detained student know she is still loved.

The most important time may be after the student is released: A friend who has worked in juvenile justice for over a decade, stresses the importance of connecting recently released youth with a positive peer support group. This can be tough, though, because most churches and groups don't want "those kids" around "our kids." This should lead to the essential question: "What would Jesus do?" Figure it out and work hard to implement it. You, the teenager, and your group will not be the same. And whether you're able to get the group to open its doors and hearts or not, remain in contact and make yourself available to the student. Your encouragement and support are vital, as is your accountability, if you've developed a solid relationship with the student.

 Respond when students are hospitalized

Hospital visits are a great opportunity for you to be there for your students and to show how much you care. However, your visit can be a burden for the patient, parents, and staff. That's why it's important to follow a few considerate steps on these visits. (P.S.: Did you remember your ID?)

Visit the nurse's station: Stop by the nurse's station to ensure that you are visiting at a good time. Ask if there are any special precautions that you need to be mindful of when entering the room. They may request protective gear be worn or special scrubbing and in-and-out procedures.

Ask to enter the room: After the nurse's station, knock on the room door and ask if you can enter. Knocking is polite and gives the patient some time to get presentable before you enter her room; plus, the patient might be asleep. Remember, patients are powerless, so give them all the respect you can to help them regain that power. And if you are unable to see the student but parents or other family see you, you still will make a big impact through your visit.

Get on their level: Being in a hospital bed is one of the most vulnerable positions. Patients are told what they can and can't do and often rely on other people for taking care of even their most basic needs. Instead of standing over someone at bedside, which can feel imposing to a patient, sit in a chair at eye level. If no chairs are available, ask if it's OK to kneel at the bedside. And if no other options are available, ask if you can sit near the foot of his bed, if you are well-acquainted with the patient and family.

Pay attention to endurance level of patient: One time I (Matt) was a patient in the hospital and my pastor came to visit me. He was genuinely trying to be a blessing, but all of a sudden I needed to vomit. Being young, I had no idea if it was OK to do that in front of a pastor. So I held it in. After what seemed like eternity, the pastor left. As soon as he'd left the room, I threw up. Remembering this, here are a couple of suggestions: First, give permission to the patient at the beginning of your visit to be in charge of the visit. If she wants you to leave so she can take care of business, that's OK. Second, keep your visit short. Patients have decreased tolerance for visitors and conversation, so keep that in mind when determining how long to stay in the room.

Talk directly to the patient: A common error people make when visiting in hospitals is acting as though the patient has lost all capacity for speech, hearing, and reason. This usually isn't the case. If you want to know how the patient is doing, ask him. Likewise, if you are wondering how mom and dad are holding up, ask them.

Ask how you can pray: Prayer is an essential part of pastoral ministry. When listening to a person share, you may get some good ideas of how you can best pray for her. However, those are still your ideas. You empower a patient when you ask if you may pray for her and what you should pray for, and it sheds more light on what her felt needs are.

Other Opportunities to Visit Students

There are other places you might visit students in times of need, such as residential treatment centers and halfway houses, psychiatric units, and rehab facilities. Make a commitment now to embrace these, even though the facility may be a substantial drive away and visiting will take a major chunk of your day. Read the other thoughts in this book and glean some of the ideas that are transferable and applicable to these visits. Your presence may be embraced or may seem unappreciated, but it can make an impact.

4 Reflections on Loss Through Death

If you're a youth worker for any length of time, you will be called on to walk with individuals and families through times of grief and loss. It could be a parent, grandparent, child, sibling, friend, or other important person in a teenager's life. These are sacred opportunities of deep ministry. You may feel awkward or may even fear your role. You may invest long hours that are physically, emotionally, and spiritually draining. But be ready to experience outcomes that cannot be adequately expressed through words. Death never comes at a convenient time. Spend time now preparing and equipping yourself for when you're called upon to respond. Some ideas:

- Talk to other seasoned Christian leaders and youth workers for ideas on the best ways to respond.

- Shadow someone ministering to a family that has experienced loss.

- Memorize or mark appropriate Scripture passages that provide comfort during times of loss.

- Tour a local mortuary, seeking to understand the services they provide, their costs and procedures, and your role respective to theirs.

- Attend multiple memorial services to build your comfort level and to get ideas.

- Create a list of local services available to assist families as they walk through the grieving process—such as local mortuaries; your church's procedures, policies, and available services related to funerals and family assistance; counselors who specialize in grief and loss; and other helpful information.

Here are additional thoughts on helping teenagers who experience loss:

63 Understand the process of loss and grief

You may be familiar with the Kübler-Ross model, also known as The Five Stages of Grief: denial, anger, bargaining, depression, and acceptance. This model is simple, predictable, and understandable, but grief is not a linear process. Not everyone experiences all of these stages or experiences them in the same order. The best we can do is to walk with a person as she experiences these emotions and normalize her feelings as she experiences them. People grieve for different periods of time after a major loss. Birthdays, anniversaries, special events, and holidays can cause a surge in the pain associated with loss. And some people need professional assistance to help them cope with their grief; this is when you can turn to the list of Christian counselors you've already compiled.

64 Be present in students' lives

Make sure teenagers and their families are not walking this journey alone. Visit and check in often. Envision what you would need if this were your journey. Arrange meals for the family. Do they need help cleaning their house, mowing their lawn, or driving family members to sports practices, doctor appointments, or the store? Maybe they need someone to talk to or to just listen to them for a few hours. Pull together a concerned team of friends and family to stand alongside them.

65 Offer comfort through presence

This is easiest if you already have a relationship established, but you also may enter the lives of total strangers. What they need now is your presence, not a professional counselor. Come with a listening ear and an empathetic, caring spirit. Respond quickly and compassionately. Scripture reading and prayer are appropriate and even welcomed by most people, no matter their view of faith or religion. Remember that you are there in the role of a pastor—even if you don't have that title or position. Platitudes and simple answers will never be enough. Survivors don't care if you think she's in a better place. That may be true, but they miss her and wish she could be back with them. It is not your role to decide the spiritual fate of the deceased, especially now. Listen, and don't be afraid to say, "I don't know." Allow them to express anger and doubt. They need your presence more than your best attempts at wise answers. Be ready and willing to help the survivors plan the remembrances. Have a file of resources available to loan them. Share from your experience, but let them make this their service. Ask if they would like you to accompany them to the mortuary. They are usually in a fog, not thinking clearly; your presence is comforting and they trust you to help them navigate the necessary arrangements.

66 Accompany the family in moving forward

The final amen has been said and the last bouquet of flowers has withered. Life now moves on for everyone else except the immediate family and closest of friends. It is important for you to remain in contact and not also leave them. Put reminders on your calendar so you remain connected to the family. Here are some ideas:

- Check in periodically to see how they're doing

- Talk to them, ask them questions, engage them in conversation, encourage others to continue their relationships and not avoid them

- Remember all the "firsts"—the first major holidays and events that are experienced without the deceased person (such as birthdays, anniversaries, Christmas, Thanksgiving, and graduations)

- Let them know they're not forgotten; call them, write on their Facebook wall, drop them a note, take them out for coffee

- Let them know that the loved one is not forgotten and that his life made a difference, no matter how long or short it might have been

- Monitor their grieving

- Connect them with support groups

- Assist them, if needed, in traversing all the practical and legal tasks (such as bank accounts, Social Security, cleaning the deceased's room, and dispersal of possessions)

Each survivor will react and move forward differently. Life will never be the same; they will establish a new normal. Don't avoid the survivors, even if you feel awkward or don't always know what to say. Allow and even encourage grieving. Expect ups and downs, including sudden, seemingly unprompted times of tears or anger. Let them know this is normal and they're not "losing it." Celebrate their highs, and walk with them through their lows. Make sure they're surrounded by loving, patient people who will walk the journey with them. Pray for them often. Help them rebuild their lives without forgetting the deceased.

6 Sex Topics You Can't Ignore

Just thinking about this section might make you squirm, but in your role as a caregiver to teenagers, you likely will encounter times when students are struggling with these topics. It's essential to remember that God created sex and that sex was designed for marriage. Here are some common sex-related topics and issues facing teenagers:

67 Dating

First, understand a family's stance on this subject and respect the parents' voice in this matter. Second, always treat dating with an eye toward its end goal: discovering characteristics that students would and would not like in a spouse, to someday find that special someone.

Talk about the emotional impacts and frustrations in dating and how much of our hearts we give in a particular relationship. Share the pain and show the pain caused when a student gives too much of his heart to another and how it can harm future relationships. Help your ministry foster a welcoming and non-threatening environment where teenagers can mature socially as well as spiritually.

 Masturbation

In this day and age, masturbation seems like it has become a non-issue. Some students will need to be taught about the impact of lust and the need for having a pure heart in order for them to recognize it as both a problem and an addictive behavior. Other students may be struggling with the guilt of this activity. In these cases, helping the student deal with guilt is a good first step. Talking him through his struggle and helping him identify where he is most tempted and most likely to act out on this behavior can help the teenager identify strategies for coping with and fleeing from this behavior. Setting up and finding an accountability partner also can help. While not excusing the behavior, being empathetic of the struggle can help a teenager remain honest and fight the temptation.

69 Pornography

Pornography debases the *Imago Dei* of the person depicted in the imagery. It also dehumanizes sex (something God created to be between two people within the boundaries of marriage) and sets up unrealistic future expectations about sex. You can assist some students in gaining ground against porn by helping them examine the feelings and drive toward using porn and exploring the side effects and negative consequences of porn. Setting up accountability and fleeing temptation are essential. Lust and developing feelings for the opposite sex are normal; temptation hits everyone. Learning how to deal with temptation will help the teenager through this.

70 Sexting[5]

According to an MTV/AP study conducted by Knowledge Networks, 24 percent of teenagers aged 14-17 have been involved in some form of sexting— the act of using your cellphone to take sexually explicit pics of yourself (or someone else) and send it on to a third person, often using the text feature on the phone. This increases to

33 percent between 18-24. For those wondering about the biblical ramifications of this, Ephesians 5:3-7 speaks specifically about Christians avoiding all sexual impurity. The consequences can be devastating if these pictures are sent out, landing on the Internet where their removal is impossible. Legal ramifications can even include being charged with a sex offense. Teaching against this is the same as teaching against other forms of sexual impurity. Often times, if you deal with this as a youth worker, it most likely will become a matter that involves police or child protection services.

 Premarital sex

Purity is God's design for us. As youth workers, we have the opportunity to help teenagers understand that sex is designed for (and greatest in) the boundaries of marriage. I (Matt) often talk of the progression of physical relationship that goes from holding hands, light kissing, light petting, heavy kissing, heavy petting, onward to sexual acts. I help my students understand that the problem with moving to higher levels on this ladder is that you quickly grow tired of them and will move on to the higher rungs. It is the way God designed sexual intimacy. Help students develop their boundaries before they get into a situation where their bodies are acting faster than their minds. Consider using a solid curriculum to address this in both a co-ed setting and a same-sex environment.

72 Teen pregnancy

A teenager comes to you and discloses she is pregnant; what do you do? First, know your legal obligations. (Are you a mandated reporter?) Second, get together with her (and with the baby's father, if possible) and listen, love, and pray, while helping her to process the next steps. Third, help the teenager break the news to her parents. Parents still form the most important support network. Fourth, be aware of and help those involved understand their options, including local organizations, ministries, and resources. Connect teenagers with the education and support they need. Fifth, support the students and parents without condoning premarital sex, supporting them through all the choices that need to be made and helping them realize God's forgiveness can prepare them for the next phase of their lives. Remember there are two individuals responsible for this pregnancy; help both recognize their responsibilities and create a plan for their future. Finally, if you are the lead youth worker, address the circumstances in youth group in a manner that does not condone the action, yet does not shun the pregnant couple and does help restore them to the community. We are called to love teenagers despite whatever sin they commit and to help them reconcile with God and their community. Don't treat certain sins differently just because the consequences happen to be more visible.

SKILLED RESPONSE

CRISIS MOMENTS

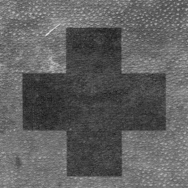

Most youth workers feel over their heads when they hear of school shootings, terrorism, natural disasters, and suicides. Being in a place where you aren't sure what to do next makes you become more reliant on God and makes you think about what you should and ought to be doing. This section offers specific strategies and thoughts on responding to crisis moments. You can never fully plan for every detail you'll encounter in these situations, but you can take steps to equip yourself and become more prepared to respond well.

6 Keys to Crisis Response

73 Can you cope with a crisis?

First rule in coping with a crisis: Don't do anything to create problems or exacerbate the situation. The second rule: The more prepared we are for crises, the better we can cope with and survive these difficult situations. Some helpful questions:

- Have you honestly sat and thought through worst-case scenarios—illness, accidents, deaths, needing to send someone home?

- Do you have permission slips (students) and medical info for everyone (including adults)?

- If traveling, have you made copies of all essential trip documents/itineraries and spread them among the leadership? Did you leave copies in the office or with a trusted leader/parent at home?

- If you are unable to be in charge, have you communicated with the team who is to take over?

The better you can answer these important questions, the better your reaction will be if something were to happen.

74 Preparation is key

Work with your ministry team to create a plan for responding to crises. Schools and other institutions often practice their crisis-response plans several times a year; learn from them. Ask how you or your church can help in the event of a crisis (such as providing counselors or opening your doors as an emergency shelter). If you aren't involved in the planning and training, you may not be welcome or effective during a real crisis. Talk with staff and volunteers about what should happen in a crisis situation, whether it's a suicidal student, someone with a gun, a natural disaster, or some other emergency. If the crisis is happening to you or your church, realize that your leadership team is going to be taxed. There are many teams that specialize in critical incident stress management across the country and a few that specialize in working with faith-based organizations. These teams are equipped to support you and your staff and to help your group. They are trained to differentiate between normal stress reactions and to provide the care you need so you don't burn out as you deal with the crisis, your group, and your own emotional and spiritual state. Enter the words CISM (Critical Incident Stress Management) or ICISF (International Critical Incident Stress Foundation) in a search engine to find local teams.

75 Don't self-deploy— though there are times when you must

Much of the response at Columbine is now the epitome of what *not* to do in a crisis. Many people self-deployed— they appointed themselves crisis counselors and went to the school, clogging the roads to the point where law enforcement couldn't get in. People entered the large park behind the school (where police were trying to restrict access) and tripled the population of the park as students were being evacuated through that area. Police wasted valuable time trying to clear each person, because they had an unknown number of shooters reported in several different locations. In crises with crime scenes, stay out! If you have contacts at the school or the scene of the crisis, call them and ask if you can help. If you don't have those contacts, sometimes texting your students and opening the doors of your church or meeting people somewhere near the event might be the best option.

76 Give loaves of bread instead of stones

In the middle of the "ask, seek, knock" portion of the Sermon on the Mount, Jesus states, *"You parents—if your children ask for a loaf of bread, do you give them a stone instead?" (Matthew 7:9).* Based on the hierarchy of needs outlined by psychology professor Abraham Maslow, people in crisis require and seek solutions for physiological and safety needs first. So in a crisis, you must ensure first that people's physical needs and safety needs are being met; we refer to this as "giving them bread." Heavy spiritualization talks to a higher-level need (self-actualization) that the individual cannot fully appreciate in the midst of a crisis; we refer to this as "handing them stones." Your presence during a crisis is a form of ministry and pre-evangelism. When students and their families know how much you care, they may dig for the reasons why you care. When it is genuine and selfless, you (or another Christian) may play a role in leading that person to faith in Christ. But don't attempt to emotionally extort someone into becoming a Christian in the midst of a crisis.

77 Understand post-traumatic stress disorder

The diagnosis of post-traumatic stress disorder (PTSD) gets thrown around way too easily following a traumatic event, and the label often causes more problems than it solves. In reality, for the first four to eight weeks following a traumatic event, it's considered acute stress. While the symptoms may be similar, the prognosis is much better. Using this information can help normalize the process and minimize fears that the individual has that he is "permanently damaged." It is normal and natural in the days and weeks following a critical incident to be jumpy, operate on a hair trigger, sleep horribly, and feel like you are always in a "fight or flight" mode. It's when these symptoms fester that professional help is needed. PTSD has two forms: acute (two to three months in duration) and chronic (more than three months in duration). PTSD often is marked by severely intrusive thoughts, avoidance of anything from the event to people in general, and the constant feeling that they are in that "fight or flight" mode and can't calm down. This causes a significant impairment in the person's ability to lead a normal, focused life. While someone dealing with PTSD requires professional help, you can still care for that person and be with him as he works through his difficulties.

Caring for yourself during a crisis: I (Matt) responded to the YWAM mass casualty shooting in Arvada, Colorado and was asked to debrief survivors. Hours were spent counseling, hearing graphic details, and responding empathically to everyone. On the third day, I noticed that I started getting lethargic, experiencing symptoms, feeling as if I were present in the shooting itself, and developing fight-or-flight symptoms. The biggest threat to caregivers is buying into the illusion that when we trudge through the biggest messes of life, God will give us a Teflon® suit so we are not affected. In reality, if we care, we internalize some of what happens around us. When engaged in this type of ministry, get help for yourself, lest you crash and burn.

78 Display compassion when working with victims

Intervention in a manner that does not retraumatize the victim is essential. The first rule is to let the police do their job. Second, if someone is reporting a fresh crime (especially rape), get medical help for the individual ASAP. Then empower the victim by asking permission to join her, sitting where she would like you to sit, at a time she wants to talk. When working through a violent episode with a victim, have her share her story, choosing what she would like to share without pushing the victim to share further than she is willing to go. Pay attention to her basic needs for safety, shelter, food, and water. After she has shared her story, educate her on the normal reactions of being a victim, including being jumpy, restless, unable to sleep, or overly sleepy. Reinforce that she is not to blame for what happened, and assert the availability of people to help her through this event.

5 Thoughts on Suicides and Suicidal Behavior

Few things are more difficult and disconcerting than when a student commits suicide—a life cut short despite all of the hope and promise that lies ahead. This tragedy strikes more times than we like, with suicide being the third leading cause of death for adolescents; for each completed suicide, it is estimated that 25 suicide attempts are made.[6] These thoughts are a basic intro on recognizing warning signs in students and responding to this important issue facing today's teenagers.

79 Understand why students consider or commit suicide

Most suicide attempts are a cry for help, a desperate plea for someone to pay attention and validate the student as being worthwhile. Suicidal teenagers feel helpless, hapless, and hopeless, unable to see healthy alternatives to their current life situation. The pain, sadness, and depression outweigh their coping skills, available support systems, and ability to make wise decisions. Unable to think clearly, they feel they have lost total control and can't see any other way out; they believe nothing will change and their future is without hope. Suicide becomes a permanent solution for their temporary problem. What are some of the risk factors?

- Previous suicide attempt (only 10 percent of people who attempt suicide will go on to complete and die by suicide yet 80 percent of people who die by suicide have made a previous attempt)[7]

- Recent suicide of a close friend or family member

- History of self-harmful behavior

- Interpersonal conflict or loss of significant relationship

- History of mobility, sense of isolation, and/or poorly developed social support system

- History of mental health illness

- Feeling unwanted

- Addictions and substance abuse

- Unhealthy fascination with risk

- Death or terminal illness of a loved one

- Major physical illness or chronic pain

- Struggles with sexual identity

- Recent disappointment, failure, rejection, or embarrassment

- Recent traumatic event or severe loss

- Bullying

- Easy access to lethal means (such as poisons, guns, other weapons)

80 Create a healthy atmosphere for teenagers

Focus on preventative maintenance. Know your students; engage in incarnational ministry, living life among them and accompanying them on their journey. Create a safe, life-giving ministry where students understand and celebrate their value as God's image-bearers. Preach and teach hope and the value of life. Love and respect all students, teaching them to do the same with each other. Listen, allowing and encouraging them to struggle with the deep issues of life. Equip students with coping skills. Know the warning signs, know how to respond, and step out of your comfort zone to help. Help students develop strong connections to their families and other support systems. Train and equip your staff, students, parents, and other church leaders in suicide prevention and response. Know your community's available helping resources before you need them.

81 Know some of the warning signs

These warning signs are especially acute if the student does not have the personal coping skills or social support system that help navigate these life difficulties:

- Threats of suicide

- Drafting a suicide note

- Previous attempt

- Preoccupation with death and dying, including as the theme of what they watch, listen to, or read

- Death preparation, including making a will, planning final arrangements, and giving away prized possessions

- Unshakable depression and lack of hope

- Feeling unwanted

- Withdrawal; lost interest in hobbies, work, school, friends and/or social activities

- Sudden and drastic change in behavior, including a decline in performance

- Extreme fatigue, moodiness, and emotional outbursts

- Lost interest in personal appearance

- Struggle with sexual identity

- Family instability and conflict

- Increased risk taking

- Increased drug and alcohol abuse

- Recent traumatic event or severe loss, including close social relationship

- Recent humiliation or failure

- Exposure to another's suicidal behavior

82 Be prepared to make a quick assessment and get involved

SLAP is a quick—though not foolproof—way to assess the level of suicide risk. Compounding factors such as alcohol, drugs, psychosis, and intentional deceit can alter the predictive ability of this tool. Read more about SLAP[8] so you better understand its use and limitations.

S   Specificity of plan (the more detailed the plan—including means, time, and location—the higher the risk)

L   Lethality of the plan (the more lethal the plan, the higher the risk)

A   Availability of the means (the more available the weapon or means of self-harm, the higher the risk)

P   Proximity to support system and helping
        resources (students with a less developed
        support system are at greater risk; plans that are
        intended to take place further from helping
        resources and potential rescuers demonstrate
        greater risk)

Watch for and take seriously the warning signs, and then
engage ASAP, ideally face-to-face. The student will not
be thinking clearly; get close, talk loud, interact more so
they know you're there. Be more directive, asking tough
questions. Ask if he plans on hurting himself, and if so,
how. Listen intently, don't act shocked, and don't lecture.
Triage, assessing the level of risk. Take notes: Symptoms?
Precipitating crisis? Current level of functioning? Personal
support system to tap into? Go for immediate reduction
of the risk. Love, accept, and empathize. Affirm and
encourage; dispense hope, not simplistic answers.
Don't be sworn to secrecy; involve others who need to
know and who can help. Remove the intended means of
suicide. Create an action plan that is concrete, realistic,
time-limited, appropriate to the student's functioning level
and dependency needs, and includes significant others
and their social network, accountability and follow-up.
Give the student your phone number and the numbers
for local and national suicide hotlines. Make her promise
to call you if she feels like committing suicide, and then

promise you'll respond. If necessary, call the police and have the student admitted to the hospital or a residential facility. Follow up and be frequently available, referring to professional care and counseling when appropriate. Inform your supervisors, seeking personal support and self-care.

83 Respond compassionately after a suicide

Each suicide intimately affects on average six other people.[9] Come alongside them as they process their shock, grief, and anger. Survivors may blame themselves, wondering what they could have done to stop the suicide. Other emotions include denial, confusion, loneliness, guilt, rejection, disbelief, and shame. Help survivors understand that their road to recovery will be long but there is hope for healing. Your goal is to help the family and community get back to normal—a new normal—and to prevent cluster or copycat suicides. Listen and be available. Connect survivors to professional help, including support groups. It's not your job to assign an eternal destiny to the deceased, but you must bring hope in Jesus Christ to the survivors. Make sure the other students understand that while people might have suicidal thoughts, this doesn't make someone crazy—and death is permanent. The student who committed suicide shouldn't be viewed as having found an appropriate solution to his problems. Ask the tough questions of survivors, assessing their level of risk and need. Don't forget your own need for support and follow-up care.

Helping Students Through 5 Other Kinds of Crises

84 Responding to self-injurious behavior

Once, when working at a summer camp, I (Matt) noticed that one of the girls was always wearing a long-sleeved shirt—whether she was outside, inside, or even in the pool. This seemed odd and out of place considering the 90-degree, high-humidity days. She was more withdrawn than usual, so I found a time when we were apart from the group to ask her if she was cutting. At first she denied it but then stated that she was and that her parents already knew. Like many who cut, she did so to escape emotional pain and often did it impulsively. She had a kit to help her not cut that she used when needed. She showed it to me; tools that would help trick her mind into thinking she cut so the same neurochemicals could be released, giving her a relieved feeling. Self-injury is often not about suicide but is an attempt to escape some form of pain, abuse, or rejection. Often the best we can do as caregivers is to affirm her and her innate value, which goes a long way. Walking with her and not judging her as she seeks healing will help her feel less ostracized. In this case, I did verify with one of her parents that they knew she cut. I also encouraged her to talk about this with her small group leader, and she received formal counseling to address the underlying issues. Cutting can be a chronic problem that requires additional counseling and may coexist with other mental health disorders.

 Responding to rape

A person who was just raped should be encouraged to go directly to the hospital without "washing up." Remember this unfortunate truth: The victim's body is considered a crime scene. If the person is willing to call 911 from where you are and have an ambulance take her (along with police) to a hospital, ask if she would like you (or someone else) to meet her in the ER (or you might be able to ride along in the ambulance). Sometimes evidence can be collected days after the event. Get your supervisor involved as well, and don't handle the situation alone. Rape is an act of violence that takes all the power away from the victim. The best way to help someone to regain her dignity is to empower her. Don't assume things that the person ought to or should feel or do. Instead, encourage her to share her story with you when she's ready. Ask permission! This puts the victim back in the driver's seat. Reinforce that this event was not her fault and nobody deserves it or has it coming. Avoid being skeptical or doubtful of the person. Let the police do the interviewing; support the victim and help her. Acknowledge and accept the many feelings the victim will experience over the coming days and months.

 Responding to abuse

The first thing you need to remember is that you are most likely considered a mandated reporter by your state. In other words, if you don't report a suspicion of abuse to the state's abuse hotline, you can be held legally liable. Abuse, especially within family systems, can be hard to combat because of the dynamics of enabling, denial, and covering up to protect the family unit regardless of the injuries that are happening. The following website can help you discern your state's requirements for reporting abuse: childwelfare.gov/systemwide/laws_policies/statutes/clergymandated.cfm

Know what abuse looks like: Symptoms of abuse can include aggression, behavioral changes, mistrust of a particular gender, social withdrawal, and depression, as well as physical injuries that often will not match the description of how the individual says they happened. Abuse is rooted in many factors, including poverty, a history of abuse in the abuser's past, and substance abuse. Helping the victim work through abuse may be difficult and often includes self-blame, denial, projection, and anger. Victims need specialized counseling, which includes reassigning the blame from the victim to the perpetrator of the abuse. If necessary, help the victim and family find a safe place away from the abuser.

87 Responding to domestic violence

Take allegations of domestic violence seriously. Victims of domestic violence will often try to escape when the target of the violence changes from them to their children. When the victim comes out with her allegation, it is the most dangerous time for the victim and those who seek to protect the victim. Families entangled with domestic violence often mask the symptoms, making the perpetrator much more believable when he denies the allegations. Many areas have shelters and places for victims to stay. Often, I (Matt) encourage restraint orders where there is clear violence and police intervention is warranted. Documentation of violence is very important for restraining orders and court reporting. Reconciliation is a long process and often involves prolonged counseling, first with the couple as separate entities and only when safety is assured. Encouraging the spouse to simply return to the partner before safety is assured is unwise. Once violence is exposed, the perpetrator might seek revenge for the significant other's betrayal. Children may also need to be removed from the home for their own safety.

Cycle of violence: Educating perpetrators and victims about the cycle of violence may help them recognize the problem and trace the pattern of this maladaptive behavior into the past. Essentially, the cycle of violence includes three events: (1) tension builds (frustrations, anger, hostility, victim withdraws, attempts to placate); (2) abusive incident (abuser lashes out, victim is traumatized, batterer blames victim for occurrence); and (3) honeymoon period (abuser is repentant, victim is ambivalent, batterer manipulates the situation and denies severity of event, victim assumes guilt of occurrence, batterer promises change, victim sees some temporal change and may recant that abuse ever happened). The honeymoon period continues until tension (1) starts building again.

88 Responding to violent acts and terrorism

Your role with a victim of violence or terrorism may be that of advocate. While justice may not solve all problems, helping a teenager regain his voice may help him not continue to be victimized. Victims of violence may take matters into their own hands if they feel nobody cares (either through striking back or self-injury, including suicide). Sometimes, when the perpetrator is in proximity to the victim, it may be impossible for the victim to build positive coping skills and start the healing process. In the case of terrorism, targets are often random, so helping teenagers feel safe in their routines is also important. Remember that along with spiritual support, the victims need to feel that their safety and physiological needs are met for healing and recovery to begin.

11 Lessons from Columbine: Thoughts on Responding to School Crises

We're (Brad) a Columbine family. We were among the many who "retook" the school in August 1999. That allowed us to share in the mixed blessing of the long road to recovery. Then, a little over a year ago, my wife experienced a shooting at her middle school. The following thoughts were formed during my experiences as a husband, father, friend, volunteer, pastor, and youth ministry educator in the middle of these crises.

 **Go!**

Now is not the time to question if you should drop everything. The important thing is to figure out where you should go. As mentioned earlier, in most cases, do not self-deploy to the site of the tragedy. You may not be able to get past police lines, and if you do you'll be in the way and perhaps in personal danger. Where are the students congregating? Where are the parents being sent? Is your church or ministry close enough to be used as a gathering place? Key response locations for Columbine were local churches and a nearby elementary school where families were being directed.

90 Observe and obey protocol

Follow the protocol established by the authorities in charge of the situation. Your role is to be available to help, not to force yourself into the situation. At my wife's school, I was not allowed to go past the police perimeter. Once the faculty, staff, and students had been evacuated to a nearby elementary school, I was allowed and even welcomed in. In contrast, a local pastor who had no relationship with the school invited himself into where everyone was staging. Not only was he unwelcome, he was also a hindrance.

Christ incarnate

As a Christ-follower, indwelt by the Holy Spirit, you are the hands and feet of God. In the words of one Columbine student, "We needed God with skin on, not theological platitudes." Practice incarnational ministry. You may or may not be wearing a WWJD bracelet, but use that standard for your actions; what *would* Jesus do? Listen. Weep. Grieve. Provide a cup of cold water. Make phone calls. Hug, if appropriate. Seek to understand both the real needs and the felt needs. Do what you can to meet them or find people who can.

 **Here now!**

Most important, be fully present. Students and their families need an encounter with the divine through relationship, not in religion. It's your fully engaged presence that matters most—more than your eloquence of speech, your highly developed skills of leadership, your gifts of planning and teaching, or any other of those things that make you a gifted youth worker.

93 Serve first

You don't have all the answers, so don't act like you do. This is difficult. We think we need to be the answer people that fix everything. Mark 3:14 tells us that Jesus chose the disciples to be his companions and to minister to people's needs—through the good, the bad, the highs, the lows, the times of joy, the difficult times of sorrow and sadness. That is our calling, as well. Come alongside without any thought of what this will cost you or how this will or won't benefit you. And this is definitely not a time to see yourself in competition with other ministries. Your response must be cooperative compassion, not closed-minded competition.

94 Relationships are key

A Columbine student, reflecting back on the official response, said, "Be there for us before the crisis strikes so we trust you in the middle of it and after." This is reminiscent of the times when parents come to me (Brad) as their child hits her teen years and say, "My daughter doesn't talk to me." What I want to say is, "Did you talk with her when she was four? Six? Eight? Ten? If not, why should she now want to make you her confidant?"

Relationships are key before the crisis strikes, during the time of crisis, and when it's in the rearview mirror. And proactively equip your students and other staff to do the same.

95 Evangelism is secondary

This is not the time to do your best Billy Graham imitation. Listen, love, serve, and pray. Allow God to work through you. If God chooses to use this time to bring people to saving faith, then that is God's role.

96 Be the rock, but...

...be aware of your own needs as a responder. Responding to crisis is physically, emotionally, and spiritually exhausting. You're of no use to anyone if you crash and burn. In fact, you may be a hindrance. Know when to step back and recharge. Find people who can come alongside you as your support team. Know your limitations of knowledge, skill, and gifting.

Embrace emotions

One Columbine student said, "Let us be emotional, even irrational." This is especially difficult for those wired like me (Brad). We're analytical, majoring in logic. We're fixers. But we need to allow and even embrace our students' range of emotions—confusion, worry, pain, anger, fear, frustration. You can't make these emotions magically disappear through your wise words and a simple prayer. Come alongside, empathize, and seek to feel people's pain, but never say you understand unless you've personally been through the same thing. It cheapens what they're feeling and hinders their acceptance of your role in entering their lives.

 **Long-haul ministry**

Individuals respond differently to crisis. Their needs are different, they heal in different ways, and they heal at different paces. Commit to settling in for the long haul. The Columbine tragedy was over a decade ago, and the healing is still ongoing. And remember, things will never "get back to normal." Healing happens, but you have to find a new normal. Those involved in tragedy come through it as changed people who we hope are healthy but who will never the same as before.

# **99** Shield and protect

Create a safe place in the midst of the crisis. This includes protecting students and their families from the media and from the "experts" who have all the answers. During the Columbine response, the head of the local youth ministry network took on the role of screening all calls and offers of help from the many individuals and ministries that thought they had the answers for responding. Many of them were sincere and had the best of motives, but they were still told that they were not needed and would be in the way of what was really needed—a safe place for the students with those they knew and trusted.

The Importance of Sacred Presence in Crisis Response

In the months following the tragedy, I (Brad) asked survivors what was the most important lesson to pass on to people who may have to respond to a crisis like the Columbine shooting. Again and again they spoke of the importance and healing power of sacred, incarnational presence. The following quotes are representative:

The best witness is with-ness.

129

Remember the ministry of one.

I didn't want to speak to someone I didn't know...no one went to the professional counselors....Our church brought in a bunch of counselors from our denomination. They sat there all day and no one went to see them....We went to our youth pastors, to our friends, to adults from our youth groups...we just wanted to be with our friends in a safe place.

This sentiment was echoed by a national newscaster who said, in an "I really don't get it" tone:

"The professional counseling community is pouring into Littleton, but the kids are flocking to the churches."

We get it. We create a sacred space when we enter into ministering relationship with students guided by, empowered, representing, and indwelt by the Spirit of the living God.

Closing Thoughts

We want to end by thanking you for loving and caring for the students in your youth group. Youth ministry can be a thankless job, and the responsibilities we carry are often heavy. Please, remember to take care of yourself, be in God's Word, and remain devoted to prayer. No matter your position in your ministry, choose to be a good listener. This will pay off no matter how else you can care for your group. Do no harm (see Mark 9:42). Admit when you're in over your head, and get help. It's OK to say, "I don't know, but let's find someone who does."

Sometimes the best any of us can do is just to be with our students in their darkest hours. Remember, these are sacred opportunities. And when you're present, the indwelling Holy Spirit of God is there, serving your students through you. Our prayer is that God uses you, your gifts, and your heart for ministry to do great things in God's kingdom.

ENDNOTES

1. preceptaustin.org/the_attributes_of_god_-_spurgeon.htm

2. Ryan and Zeran, 1972, *Organizational and Administration of Guidance Services*. Danville, IL, Interstate Printers and Publishers.

3. J.A. Ewing, "Detecting Alcoholism: The CAGE Questionnaire," Journal of the American Medical Association (1984), 1905-1907.

4. James O. Prochaska, John Norcross, and Carlo DiClemente, *Changing for Good* (New York: William Morrow, 1994).

5. MTV/AP, *A Thin Line: About Us*, September 29, 2009. Retrieved August 11, 2011, from A Thin Line: MTV's sexting, cyberbullying, digital dating abuse campaign (athinline.org/about#research).

6. American Association of Suicidology. suicidology.com

7. Feeling Blue Suicide Prevention Council, "After an Attempt: The Emotional Impact of a Suicide Attempt." feelingblue.org

8. ssw.umich.edu/simulation/rube-assessmentScales. pdf

9. American Association of Suicidology. suicidology.com